THE Lemonheads

Mick St Michael

OMNIBUS PRESS
LONDON / NEW YORK / PARIS / SYDNEY

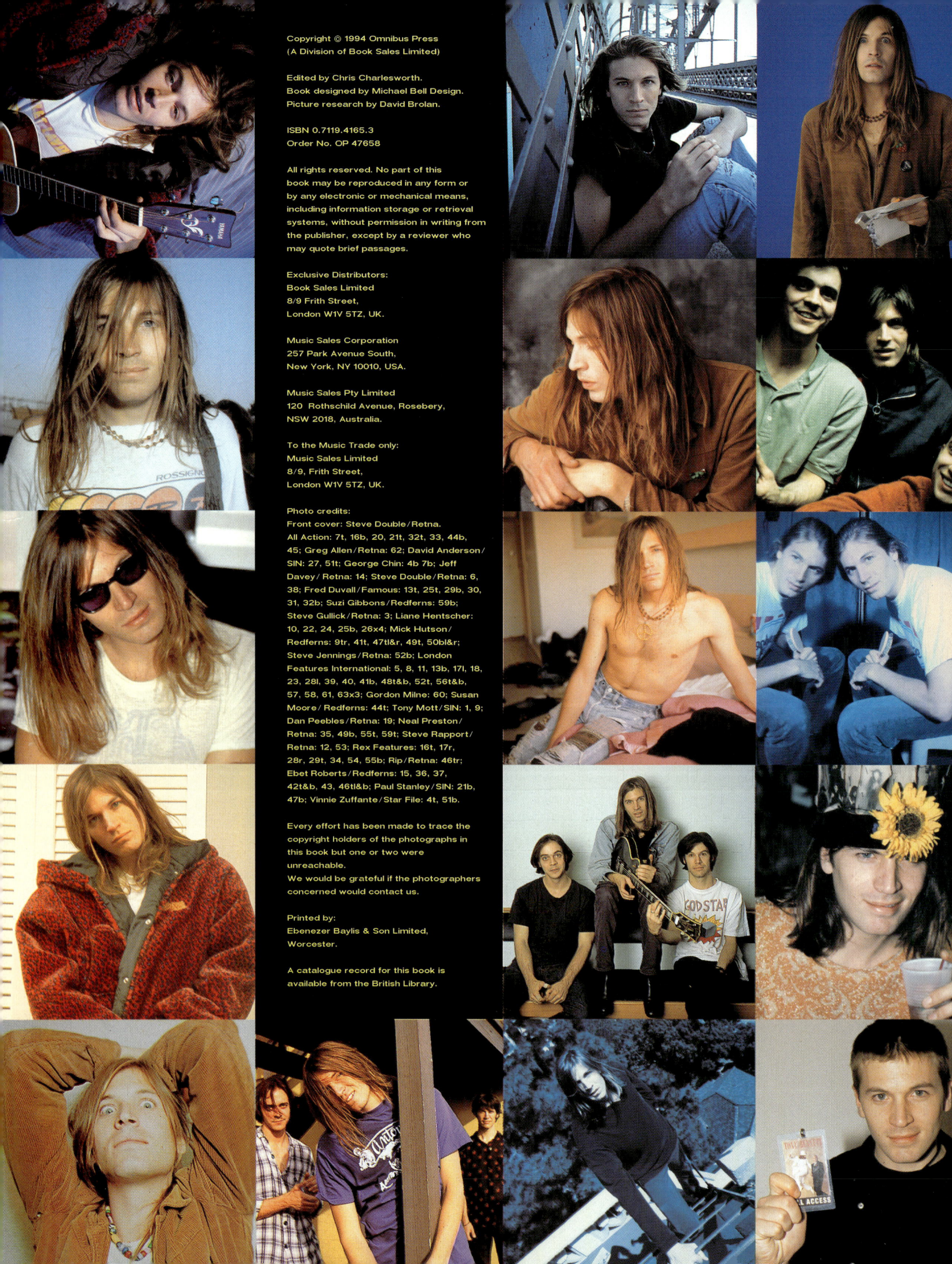

Copyright © 1994 Omnibus Press
(A Division of Book Sales Limited)

Edited by Chris Charlesworth.
Book designed by Michael Bell Design.
Picture research by David Brolan.

ISBN 0.7119.4165.3
Order No. OP 47658

All rights reserved. No part of this book may be reproduced in any form or by any electronic or mechanical means, including information storage or retrieval systems, without permission in writing from the publisher, except by a reviewer who may quote brief passages.

Exclusive Distributors:
Book Sales Limited
8/9 Frith Street,
London W1V 5TZ, UK.

Music Sales Corporation
257 Park Avenue South,
New York, NY 10010, USA.

Music Sales Pty Limited
120 Rothschild Avenue, Rosebery,
NSW 2018, Australia.

To the Music Trade only:
Music Sales Limited
8/9 Frith Street,
London W1V 5TZ, UK.

Photo credits:
Front cover: Steve Double/Retna.
All Action: 7t, 16b, 20, 21, 32t, 33, 44b, 45; Greg Allen/Retna: 62; David Anderson/SIN: 27, 51t; George Chin: 4b 7b; Jeff Davey/Retna: 14; Steve Double/Retna: 6, 38; Fred Duvall/Famous: 13t, 25t, 29b, 30, 31, 32b; Suzi Gibbons/Redferns: 59b; Steve Gullick/Retna: 3; Liane Hentscher: 10, 22, 24, 25b, 26x4; Mick Hutson/Redferns: 9tr, 41t, 47tl&r, 49t, 50bl&r; Steve Jennings/Retna: 52b; London Features International: 5, 8, 11, 13b, 17l, 18, 23, 28l, 39, 40, 41b, 48t&b, 52t, 56t&b, 57, 58, 61, 63x3; Gordon Milne: 60; Susan Moore/Redferns: 44t; Tony Mott/SIN: 1, 9; Dan Peebles/Retna: 19; Neal Preston/Retna: 35, 49b, 55t, 59t; Steve Rapport/Retna: 12, 53; Rex Features: 16t, 17r, 28r, 29t, 34, 54, 55b; Rip/Retna: 46tr; Ebet Roberts/Redferns: 15, 36, 37, 42t&b, 43, 46tl&b; Paul Stanley/SIN: 21b, 47b; Vinnie Zuffante/Star File: 4t, 51b.

Every effort has been made to trace the copyright holders of the photographs in this book but one or two were unreachable.
We would be grateful if the photographers concerned would contact us.

Printed by:
Ebenezer Baylis & Son Limited,
Worcester.

A catalogue record for this book is available from the British Library.

THE Lemonheads

Mick St Michael

From Orange Juice to The Virgin Prunes, the rock scene has seen its share of fruity groups. So when a band out of Boston, Massachusetts, called The Lemonheads released their first EP, 'Laughing All The Way To The Cleaners', on a local label in 1986, barely an eyebrow of interest was raised. Few would have predicted that they would go on to make their mark with a trio of albums that lit up the Nineties like a firework display... let alone the fact that lead singer, guitarist and songwriter Evan Griffith Dando would get his face onto hundreds of magazine covers and thousands more bedroom walls from Brighton to Baltimore.

Defining the X factor that separated The Lemonheads from their less successful contemporaries in the late-Eighties indie charts and saw them graduate to greatness has, inevitably, got a whole lot to do with Dando. Yet this is a man who delights in laying false trails, confusing his interviewers beyond belief and sending out highly contradictory messages to his public.

We wind back to the early Eighties when two Boston schoolkids got together and started to explore the world of music. One, naturally enough, was Dando, the other English Literature student Ben Deily. Both shared a love of the New Wave, both the imported variety from Britain and recent home-grown acts of the guitar persuasion like The Replacements. What might come as something of a surprise though is that, at that time, Evan Dando fancied himself as a drummer!

With Deily on guitar and vocals, they searched for a musician or musicians to complete a band – and found Jesse Peretz by the simple and (for The Lemonheads) relatively straightforward means of co-opting him from the Commonwealth High School jazz ensemble.

The newly-born trio, at this point unfortunately christened The Whelps ("you know, like a little dog," as Dando tells interviewers), donated their first couple of recordings to a school project. Reading between the lines a little, this supreme sacrifice was made merely to gain access to the institution's four-track tape recorder. So far, these have yet to see the light of day on bootleg, but it's only a matter of time...

Indeed, the results were encouraging enough for them to have a second try in a 'proper' studio, and this they did mere days after graduating in mid 1986. Mind you, since Dando once listed his most regrettable sexual experience as 'sleeping with my maths teacher at high school', perhaps he was fortunate not to have been expelled!

Home life for the young Evan was somewhat confused, too. Born on March 4, 1967, he'd been an early arrival in the legendary Summer of Love, but domestic harmony between his lawyer father and fashion model mother was not, he claims, always apparent. "I was really messed over when I was little," he revealed years later in one of many psycho-analytical interviews. "When I was eleven my parents got divorced and the song 'Confetti' (released on 'It's A Shame About Ray') was like a weird exorcism of all the anger that I had, finally getting it out of my system."

It hadn't always been that way, though. "My parents were like this perfect couple," Evan explained. "They were even in commercials on television. It was like, 'Oh, Susan and Jeff are the perfect couple, Jeff's so easy going.' The thing was, inside, he wasn't going along with it. And so he snapped, he just took off...

"And then I had a sister, right? And she got to hang out with my mom a lot. We had this apartment with a long hall in it, and I was down one end and my sister and my mom were down the other. And I was alone at that crucial age of about 11 or 12 and that just confused me even more. I didn't register what kind of pain I was experiencing."

against just one written by his partner. The odd song out was a cover version of 'I Am A Rabbit', an obscure 1978 song by an Antipodean punk band rejoicing in the name of Proud Scum. This potentially embarrassing throwback ("I am a rabbit/I have to have it") would resurface later in The Lemonheads' career...

Ironically, too, it was to be this last-named track that would attract the interest of Curtis Casella, a local DJ then in the process of launching his own record label. The Whelps were understandably keen he should release the entire session, but Casella was so short of cash they had to agree to pay for its manufacture themselves! Four of the tracks – the aforementioned 'Rabbit', plus 'Glad I Don't Know', 'I'd Like To' and Deily's wry 'So I Fucked Up',

He kept in touch with his father, but was clearly and understandably unsettled. Yet, cynics might retrospectively muse, of such cruel deprivations are successful singer-songwriters made. At other times, Dando has been said to be both a relation of a pioneer synthesiser manufacturer and a descendant of Dubose Heyward, who wrote the lyrics to the classic 'Summertime' ("And the living is easy...", etc). The latter seems more likely, given the tenor of his lyrics and the reality of his music, but it all certainly adds to the mystique.

Evan was already interested in the guitar, and was happy to take turn and turn about with Deily on their respective songs. And of the five they committed to tape with release in mind, three were Dando compositions as

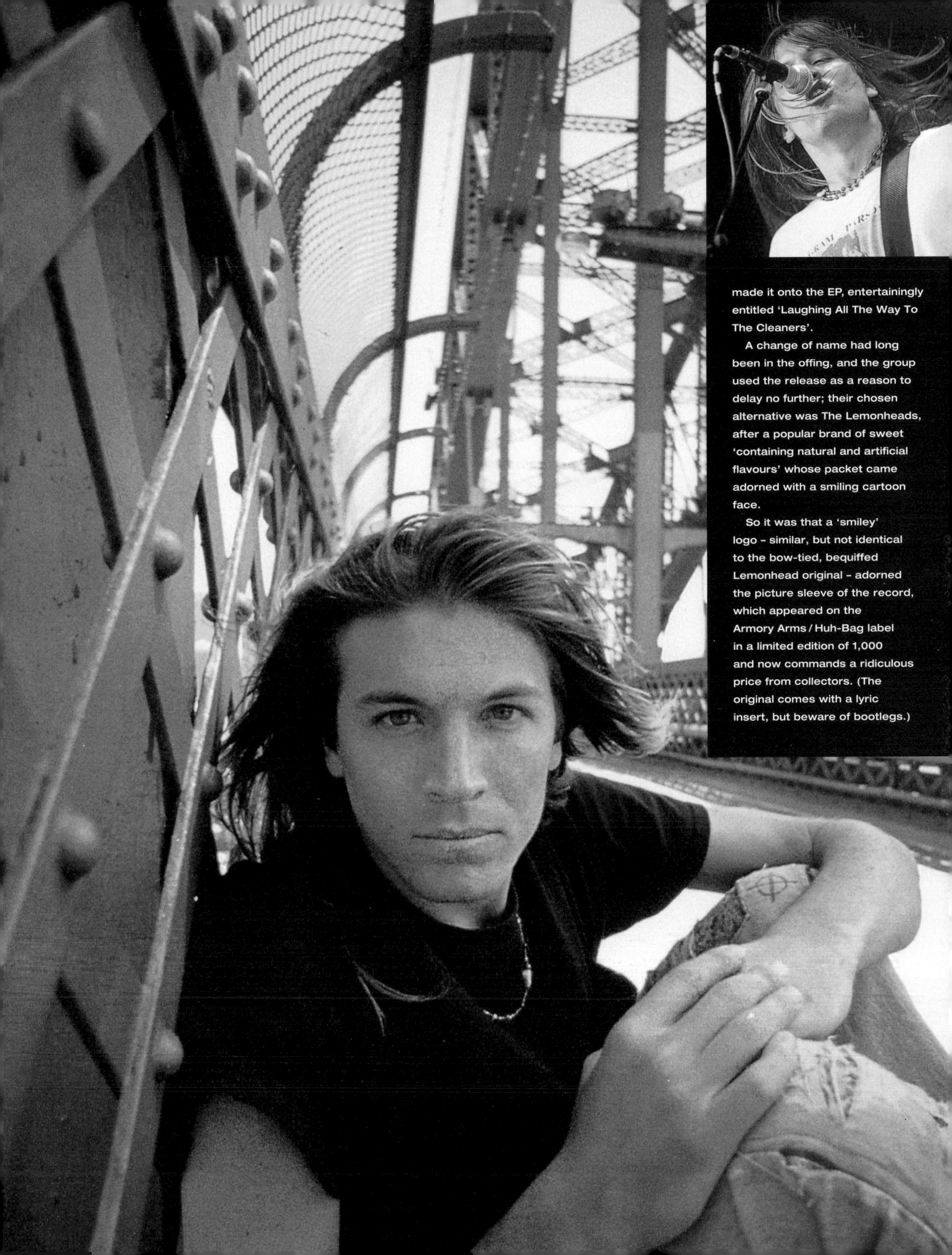

made it onto the EP, entertainingly entitled 'Laughing All The Way To The Cleaners'.

A change of name had long been in the offing, and the group used the release as a reason to delay no further; their chosen alternative was The Lemonheads, after a popular brand of sweet 'containing natural and artificial flavours' whose packet came adorned with a smiling cartoon face.

So it was that a 'smiley' logo – similar, but not identical to the bow-tied, bequiffed Lemonhead original – adorned the picture sleeve of the record, which appeared on the Armory Arms / Huh-Bag label in a limited edition of 1,000 and now commands a ridiculous price from collectors. (The original comes with a lyric insert, but beware of bootlegs.)

The EP was also as good a reason as any for the newly rechristened band to make their first tentative steps onto the concert stage, and they soon became a familiar sight on the local club circuit. It was a Cinderella-esque situation, since with college on the not so distant horizon for all three members the trio's life-span looked a distinctly limited one.

Come the start of a new academic year, Jesse and Ben headed to the local seat of learning, Harvard, while Evan ventured further afield to Skidmore in New York State. But his academic career was destined to be short and not particularly sweet. "When I went to college, I got 0.32, that was my grade point average. That's one D and three Fs. I did one term and then I left. I could have been thrown out, but slyly I slipped a note of resignation under the office door, packed everything into my car and just drove off into a snowstorm."

On his return, he discovered that while he was busy missing lectures The Lemonheads had become an acquired taste for a surprising number of Boston music fans. Meanwhile, he'd lost the taste for playing drums, and Doug Trachten was recruited to take his place behind the kit as

the group began recording their first album. This, entitled 'Hate Your Friends', was released on the Taang! label in June 1987, by which time the punkily-coiffeured Trachten had departed. "Evan and Jesse were into having a restrained appearance," Ben Deily later suggested.

According to Record Collector magazine, 'Hate Your Friends' emerged in "roughly 70 versions, all with different combinations of vinyl colour, label colour and cover design." In Britain, World Service picked up on the album for release in May 1988. Completist collectors will doubtless drive themselves to the brink of bankruptcy trying to add the blue vinyl German edition and the yellow Australian pressing to their collection, but for those who are more interested in the music the outlook is a little better.

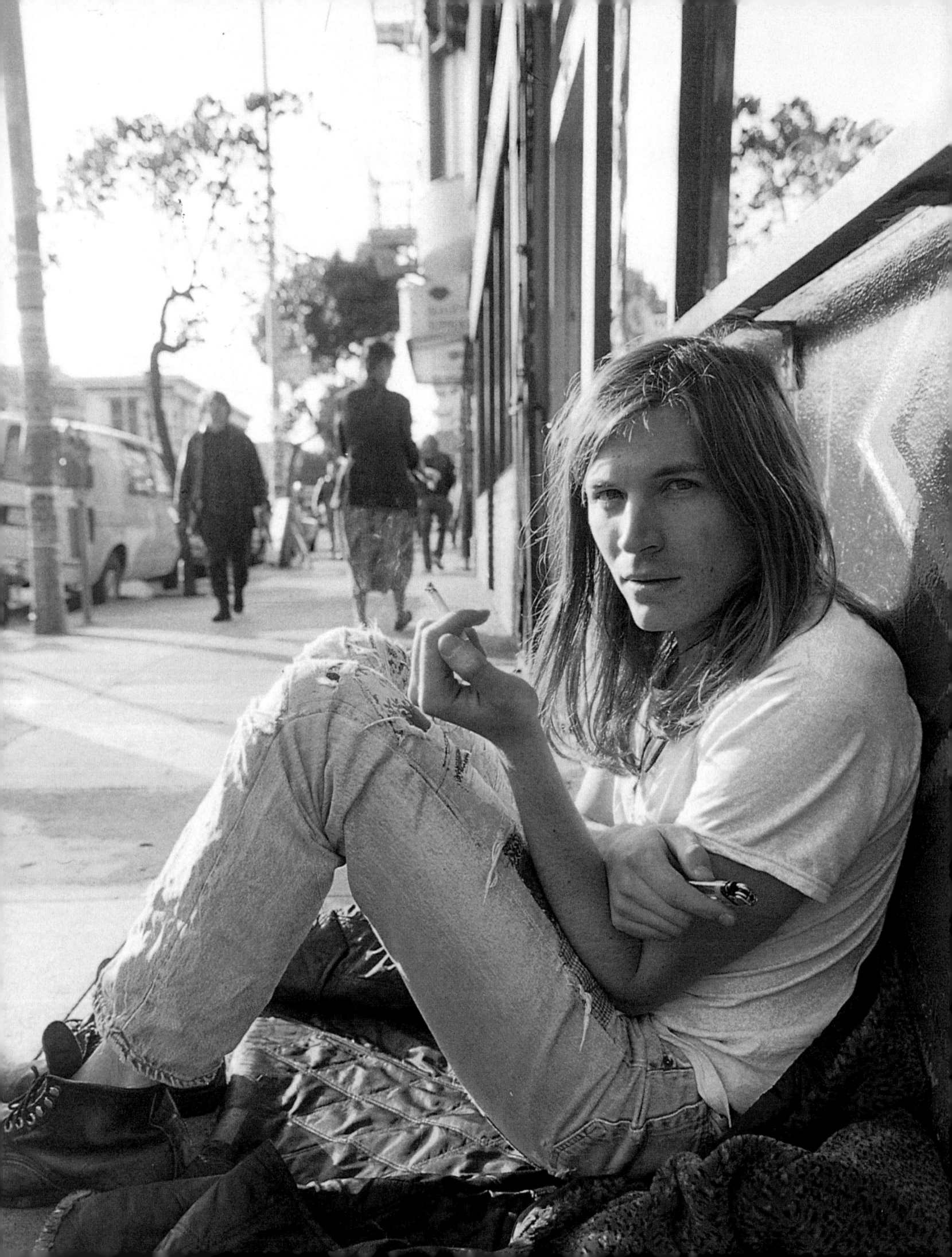

The Lemonheads' sound at this formative stage was both entertaining and erratic, veering as it did from the hardcore guitar-driven rock of 'Belt' and 'Sneakyville' to the title track and 'Don't Tell Yourself', both of which were infinitely more melodic and a pointer to things to come. The band members seem to have been aware of this lack of focus because two songs, 'Sad Girl' and 'Ever', were omitted from the final release – only to turn up later on the 'Lick' album. Surprisingly, though, Dando (by his own admission a youthful Black Sabbath fan), was keener on the heavy tracks. Ben Deily called the excluded songs "... poppy and zappy, but at that time Evan and Jesse didn't like poppy and zappy."

If you sniffed just a hint of musical differences there then your nose didn't lead you astray. For now, though, the album (originally to be titled 'Six') was approved for release, named after one of its better tracks and wrapped – in some cases, at least – in a Peretz-designed black and white sleeve.

The band couldn't venture too far from home with two students in their ranks, but an amazing stroke of luck took their fame much further afield via the marvel of television. A video for 'Second Chance', one of the standout tracks, got an airing on MTV and made them the overnight darlings of the indie set.

This fact was proved beyond doubt when they were invited to contribute a track to a Boston punk sampler called 'Crawling From Within', and decided to cover 'Mod Lang', a track originally cut by Alex Chilton's cult power-popsters Big Star. Despite the quality of their own songwriting, The Lemonheads would cover others' songs, often with devastating effect.

With all this local, bordering on national, notoriety a second album was naturally mooted – and with rhythm a priority John Strohm (borrowed from The Blake Babies) was added to the drummerless Deily-Dando-Peretz line-up for the purpose of recording. The result was 'Creator', released by Taang! in September 1988 (keen-eyed readers will note that The

Lemonheads' releases tended to follow recordings made in the summer vacation). But tensions were mounting within the group between the two main songwriters, and the album again reflected a certain lack of direction.

Deily's arty fascination with the likes of American poet Emily Dickinson hardly sat easily with cover versions of Kiss songs ('Plaster Caster') as mooted by Evan. And when he cut a version of 'Your Home Is Where You're Happy', a song originally performed by Charles Manson, the notorious killer convicted in 1970 for his involvement in the murder of, amongst others, the actress Sharon Tate, the writing was clearly on the wall for Lemonheads Mark 1. (Other less than easy listening cuts on the album included 'Clang Bang Clang' and 'Burying Ground'.)

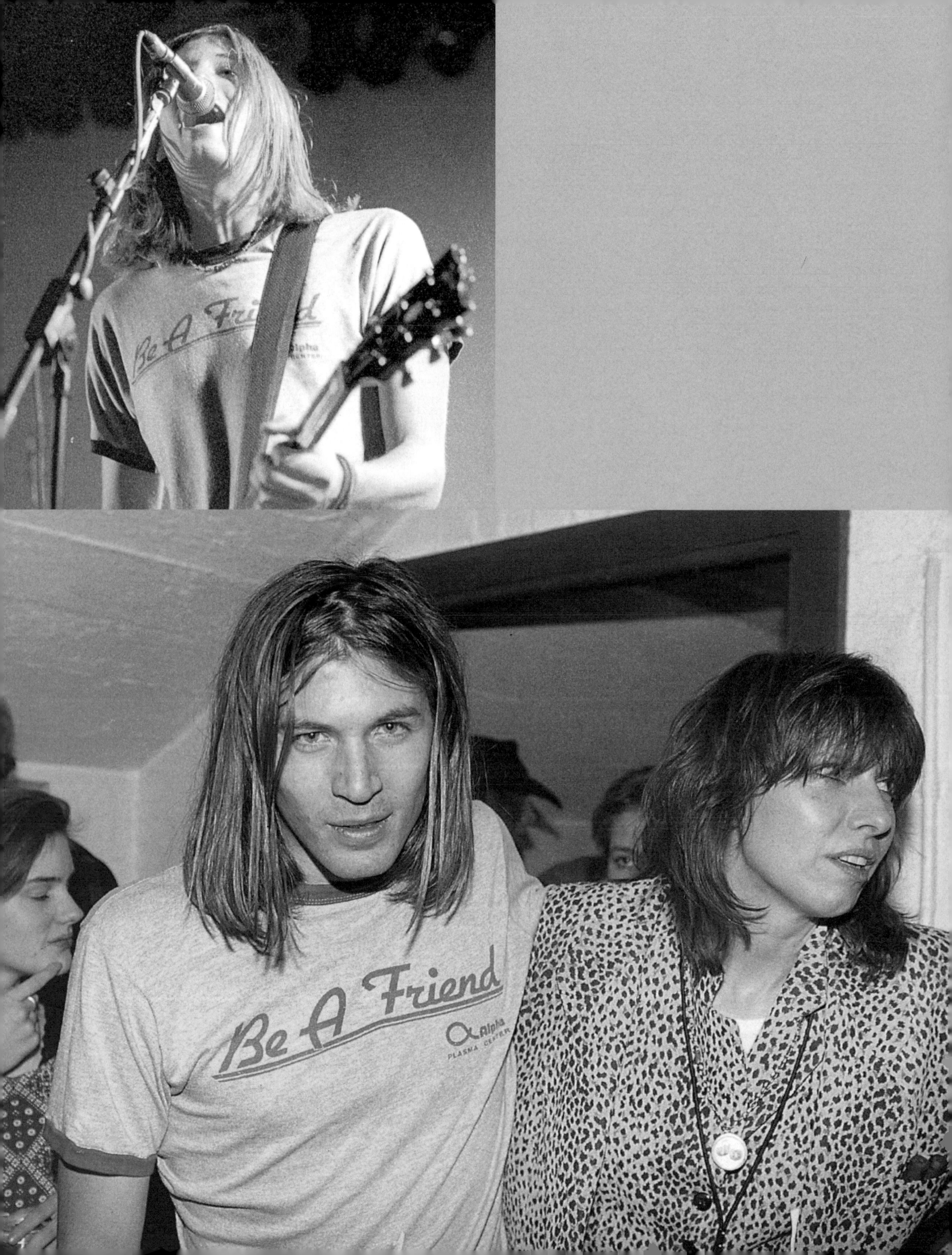

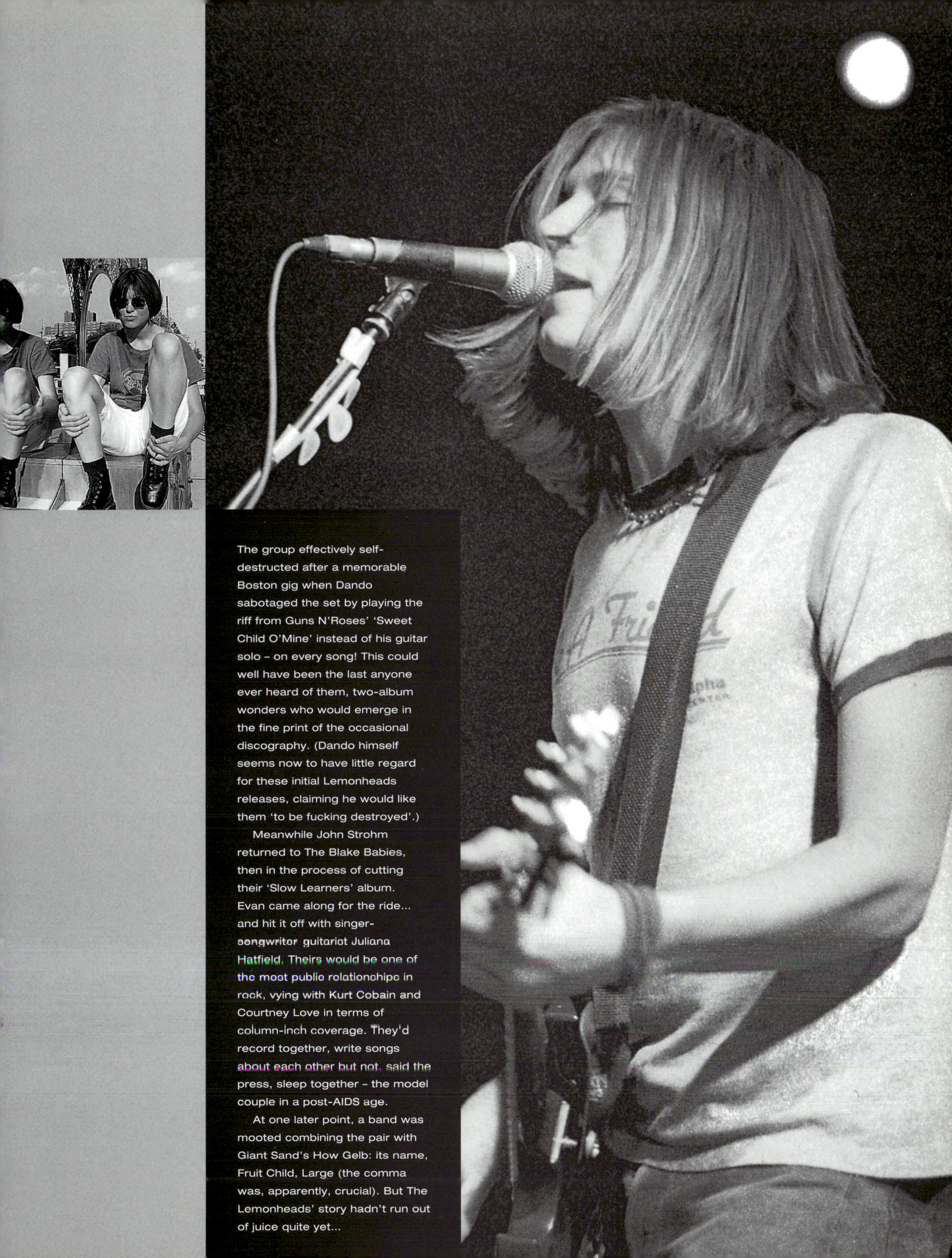

The group effectively self-destructed after a memorable Boston gig when Dando sabotaged the set by playing the riff from Guns N'Roses' 'Sweet Child O'Mine' instead of his guitar solo – on every song! This could well have been the last anyone ever heard of them, two-album wonders who would emerge in the fine print of the occasional discography. (Dando himself seems now to have little regard for these initial Lemonheads releases, claiming he would like them 'to be fucking destroyed'.)

Meanwhile John Strohm returned to The Blake Babies, then in the process of cutting their 'Slow Learners' album. Evan came along for the ride... and hit it off with singer-songwriter guitarist Juliana Hatfield. Theirs would be one of the most public relationships in rock, vying with Kurt Cobain and Courtney Love in terms of column-inch coverage. They'd record together, write songs about each other but not, said the press, sleep together – the model couple in a post-AIDS age.

At one later point, a band was mooted combining the pair with Giant Sand's How Gelb: its name, Fruit Child, Large (the comma was, apparently, crucial). But The Lemonheads' story hadn't run out of juice quite yet...

Over in Europe, echoes of the US hardcore explosion were being felt – and The Lemonheads' name was among those being mentioned in dispatches. None of the group members had involved themselves in any long-term musical projects since the split, so when a Dutch booking agency expressed interest as 1989 dawned they decided to give it another shot. This time, though, Dando was once again behind the drum kit, yielding his front-line place to a supposedly more impressive performer in Coorey Loog Brennan from a cult band called Bullet Lavolta.

With a tour confirmed, the newly constituted Lemonheads decided they'd record some new material before leaving – some people have said this was funded by winning a local Battle of the Bands, others suggested it was

an attempt to get out of their contract with their label Taang! – and, true to form, that was where the problems started. When eight weeks of recording failed to yield enough good new material to put an album together, Dando was compelled to look backwards to the future. And surprisingly enough, the most fertile source of inspiration was the band's first EP, by now some two years old. 'Glad I Don't Know' and 'I Am A Rabbit' were both re-recorded, while 'Mad', the fifth song from those first sessions which had been squeezed off the EP, was taken down from the shelf and dusted off.

While scouting for out-takes, they also discovered 'Sad Girl' and 'Ever' from the 'Hate Your Friends' sessions, and these were pressed into service alongside a newly-recorded classic 'Mallo Cup' (another product of Dando's confectionery fixation). Two cover versions also featured strongly: 'Strange', plucked from the repertoire of departed country diva Patsy Cline and 'Luka', a recent hit from the very much alive Suzanne Vega.

Against all odds, the album that emerged – punningly entitled 'Lick' – was hailed as a masterpiece. But the departure of Ben Deily, who decided all the aggravation simply wasn't worth it any more, threw the creative mantle firmly on Evan Dando's none too secure shoulders. Deily's decision to put his studies first was made despite the fact that 'Luka' was making waves in Britain, where an enraptured New Musical Express described it as 'an endearing hatchet job, a lazy, hazy melody with a gruff vocal and spiked edges.' The accompanying video was a flickering, shadowy affair which added further mystique, and all this helped sell an album which had, like its predecessors, been picked up by Rough Trade's World Service offshoot.

The track was far from the

highlight of 'Lick', but – not for the only time, as things transpired – it illustrated the fact that a well chosen cover version could open doors. For Ben Deily, though, the route to pop stardom remained firmly blocked... for now, at least. It wasn't until 1993 that he surfaced again musically, leading a group called The Pods.

His contribution to The Lemonheads' success so far had been as much on the instrumental as the songwriting fronts – his guitar playing was streets ahead of his converted drummer pal – but though his straightforward songs were in the minority quantity-wise, they complemented Dando's dreamy confections admirably. He would undoubtedly be missed – but

by exactly how much was still open to debate.

What was certain was that his departure left the spotlight firmly trained in one direction and one direction only. And when Europe called, Evan answered. A series of less than successful dates in which he'd doubled as drummer and singer had strongly suggested that Dando was better off standing up. Buckling on his trusty Gibson and stopping only to train up a substitute sticksman (Mark somebody or other, his name remains unrecorded), he led the band on the promised tour, stopping off at the BBC's Maida Vale studios to record the accolade all bands seek but only some attain – a Peel Session for Radio 1.

Recorded on 4 July and broadcast just ten days later, the session comprised spirited renditions of 'Clang Bang Clang', 'Circle Of One', 'The Door' and 'Mallo Cup'. Producer for the session was Dale Griffin, better known as Buffin, drummer for Seventies glam-rock legends Mott The Hoople.

Sadly he couldn't be pressed into service when The Lemonheads' new drummer suddenly quit halfway through an American tour, but David Ryan stepped into the breach... and remains there today. Acquired on a free transfer from a bakery shop, he rejoiced in the nickname of Dave Donuts. "I know everything about baking," he insisted, "puff pastry, croissants..." He'd apparently learned his trade

from a convict on the run called Mario, who "was wanted in 12 states for armed robbery and some kind of awful assault... he was one of the best bakers in the world."

One day the cops found Mario, and devoid of his mentor Dave adopted Evan Dando as his new guiding light. "He's good at being a frontman," said this

latest recruit of the Lemon in chief, though he also admitted that "he's a space cadet at times… but pretty bright, too." Their new recruit was quickly flown from Boston to Los Angeles, where the band were playing, and shown the ropes – his journey made possible courtesy of one of the band's first royalty cheques. A cover version of ex-Monkee Mike Nesmith's 'Different Drum' was lead track on the 'Favourite Spanish Dishes' EP, a release "just for Europe so people would have something new to get hold of… we knew we wouldn't have the LP ready in time." The B-side, 'Paint', was a song describing a shut-up shop that Dando seemed keener on than 'Drum' itself. "It's a metaphor for a person," he explained. "Inanimate objects induce sadness in me like nothing else."

Quickly installed as New Musical Express Single of the Week in mid 1990, this started gaining them the attention Dando had craved. And not merely for the Monkee connection, but because the EP's third song, 'Ride With Me', quoted Manson again. Never since The Smiths and the Moors murders had such a furore resulted, and it was one the singer milked to the full. 'When he was a little kid he was put in a boys' home so he was always against everybody because he was gypped so badly. He had an interesting view of the world because he was always an outcast,' protested Evan, who proclaimed an 'empathy' with him. The EP came out as a three-tracker in Britain on Fire Records' Roughneck subsidiary, but the darlings of the indie scene were soon to make their move.

It was about time The Lemonheads took the pop business seriously, and in the spring of 1990 signed to Atlantic Records, home at various times of Led Zeppelin, Ray Charles and Crosby, Stills and Nash among others. Not that this phased Dando in the slightest. In his words, 'The new album's in keeping with Lemonheads tradition. It's really erratic and all over the place.'

Many critics sneered at the major label's second attempt to corner the cult-rock market: the first had been five years ago with Hüsker Dü, a band as talented as The Lemonheads but one that seemingly couldn't survive being marketed the Atlantic way. It was also said that the contract binding The Lemonheads ran to 57 pages! While the American public waited, Atlantic re-vamped 'Favourite Spanish Dishes' for the US market: this is now a collector's item.

The band themselves were well aware of the dangers. "In terms of America, the majors are really trying to become credible," Jesse Peretz commented. "That's why they're signing these bands. They're not thinking, 'Oh, the Lemonheads are going to make us really rich', they're thinking 'The Lemonheads are going to make us look like we're willing to experiment. But everyone's going to go to a major now...'."

'Lovey' was released in October 1990, and served notice that The Lemonheads had survived Ben Deily's departure with some style. Yet even Evan couldn't have expected the success that would result from a mixture of country-rock ('Half The Time' and a cover version of Gram Parsons' 'Brass Buttons'),

soft rock ('Year Of The Cat') and Jonathan Richman-esque whimsy ('Stove'). 'Clang Bang Clang', the 'Creator' track whose title was taken from a Charles Manson song, was re-worked as 'Left For Dead', adding a welcome touch of subversion to the mixture, while a strange (female) answerphone message rounded off proceedings in suitably cryptic style.

Producer of the album was one Paul Q Kolderie, a man who's worked with acts as influential as Hole, Dinosaur Jr and Buffalo Tom. He revealed to Melody Maker some of Dando's tricks of the trade, explaining that, like Buffalo Tom's Bill Janovitz, "Evan uses two Marshall half-stacks, using one for rhythm and then kicking in the other one for lead and the extra power you need." Not that Evan was exactly the world's speediest guitar player, according to the man behind the glass. "Evan's great and he's pretty much got his own style, (but) they brought in an old friend of theirs to play some super speedy lead guitar because Evan can't do so much of that!"

The album was more or less a Dando solo effort, with help as required from Ryan, Perez, Juliana Hatfield and one-time Head Coorey Loog Brennan (the old friend mentioned above, who apparently quit music to become a classics professor at a girls' college). Its idiosyncrasies made a record you either loved or hated but fans and critics alike were left in little doubt that this was now very much Evan Dando's show.

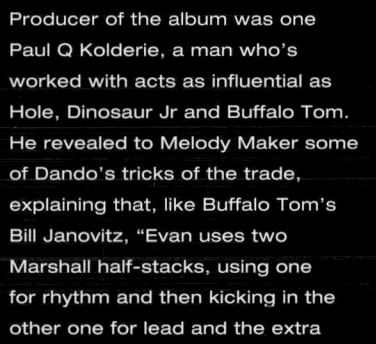

▼ JULIANA HATFIELD

But there had to be a band to promote it – and the departure of founder member Jesse Peretz in the middle of a British tour in Leeds was both unexpected and unsettling. He had designed all the band's sleeves to date, and so was very much part of their image in a visual as well as a musical way. And it had been a family affair in more ways than one; his sister had been depicted on the cover of 'Luka', his brother on the cover of some versions of 'Hate Your Friends'.

His decision to concentrate on his film degree left The Lemonheads in several degrees of confusion and it took a trip to Australia for Evan Dando to reorganise The Lemonheads. In Australia he would team up with a pair of local musicians and 'It's A Shame About Ray' would be the eventual result.

Though cut in Boston, it could have been subtitled 'What Evan Dando Did On His Holidays' – an engaging album of musical snapshots, full of local colour. He found a willing co-writer in Tom Morgan, who played in a band called Sneeze: the title track and 'Bit Part' were the first results of this fruitful musical collaboration. Slightly more obliquely, he borrowed a song, 'Frank Mills', from the Sixties hippie musical Hair – and it's either a compliment or a condemnation of the rest of the album to say that if you hadn't spotted the composer credits (or weren't over 40) you'd probably not have noticed.

The album weighed in at just over 29 minutes – a mere EP in the compact disc age of seventy-minutes-plus epics. But fans were far from short-changed in emotional terms, for this album chronicled the rebirth of a rare rock talent. "It saved my life, man," said Dando of his Australian jaunt. "The really happy songs come from Down Under. It's the distance and Valium feel of the country. The nature and solitude. I'm thinking of getting a place in Australia." (He'd successfully repeat the trick for The Lemonheads' next album.)

Bassist Nic Dalton, who also hooked up with the chief Lemonhead, expressed things from a third-party standpoint. "I just think we gave him that extra thing that music's fun," he commented. "If you listen to 'Lovey' you don't know what sort of area the music's going into, but with 'Ray' it's definitely a focused record and that's what gave it the magic. He started writing fun songs..."

For those who couldn't afford to emigrate, 'It's A Shame About Ray' was the ultimate musical trip... in more ways than one! 'My Drug Buddy' was written about exploring Sydney with a friend's girlfriend while under the influence, while 'Alison's Starting To Happen' also owed its inspiration to Ecstatic substances and another girlfriend-of-a-friend, Godstar singer Alison Galloway. "You know that weird vertigo feeling? And she went woo-ooh, and it was like, Alison's starting to happen. So I turned it into a love song, because it's a good way of describing when you fall in love, it's like something's crystallising."

Writing about people, he explained, was becoming something of a habit. "It's easier when I've been away from people for a while and I notice this fingerprint they've left on my brain... it's a good feeling, especially if you miss somebody. It's a way of bringing them back to you."

And that was certainly true of 'It's About Time', a song since openly dedicated to his 'close friend' Juliana Hatfield. Evan saw no reason to hide the fact. "Maybe one person in 20 will be interested in what's behind it. I played it for her on the telephone, and she likes it, so I got the OK. I wouldn't record it if she didn't like it."

'Hannah And Gabi' was another relationship song – and one complex enough to qualify for any Australian soap opera. "Gabi, this Australian model, allowed me to get away from Hannah and I felt disappointed with myself. But I didn't really want Gabi, either – she was a symbol of what I was missing. And before that there was this girl Louisa, who

▼ ON STAGE WITH JULIANA HATFIELD

I got away from. I want to stop getting away from everybody. I want to find the right girl." Drummer David Ryan admits this is a song that, more often than not, makes him shed a tear as he plays it live.

Amidst all this angst, Dando had, as one critic put it, discovered "a more restrained way of writing and arranging

his songs, involving proper tunes and an acoustic guitar." A trifle patronising, perhaps, but uncannily accurate.

Another magazine christened the Heads' frontman "the most eligible man in rock". Yet the man who denied that he and Juliana were an item seemed to like the idea of being a sexless pop star. In late 1993, he said "I haven't had a girlfriend for two years, and maybe once every month or two I'll have sex with someone. I've gone six months without having sex in the last year. It's not that my sex drive is low, but I can't just have sex with someone I don't even like."

'It's A Shame About Ray' was recorded at Los Angeles' Cherokee Studios, on the edge of Hollywood, and was produced by the three brothers Robb. Superstars like Steely Dan, Rod Stewart and John Cougar Mellencamp had recorded hits there, but 'Ray' was to prove as significant as any of them – eventually.

He'd recorded the album with the help of David Ryan and Juliana Hatfield, but when he tried to recruit a new group, he found problems a-plenty. "The other guys didn't work out right. We had the drummer who used to be in Squirrelbait and he just went nuts all the time. It didn't suit some of our songs which require a little more backbone, a little more Charlie Watts than an epileptic Mitch Mitchell."

Meanwhile Jesse Peretz was prepared to let bygones be bygones and give the band another shot. "We had some personal differences," said Jesse, "but we worked them out."

The first fruits of the (re)union was another manic cover version, this time a thrash through Patience And Prudence's twee classic 'Gonna Get Along Without Ya Now' – a song that hit in 1957, one whole decade before Dando's birth. Christened 'The Patience And Prudence EP' for reasons that hardly need elaboration, it was accompanied by, among

others, a cover of 'Step By Step', a track better associated with terminally unhip US teen idols New Kids On The Block. The intention of the bizarre pairing was, said Dando, "to put ourselves at the mercy of the meanest critics around to see just how slagged we can get."

They didn't get slagged, but neither did they trouble the chart compilers – and when the British public found they could get along without the single 'It's A Shame About Ray', which reached Number 70 only to sink like a stone, Atlantic Records must have wondered if they'd drawn the booby prize in the raffle. They were still trying to get their head round the fact that despite its many qualities they'd been unable to shift as many copies of 'Lovey' as their indie predecessors had shovelled copies of 'Lick' across the counter. Indeed, the near three-to-one ratio – 11,000 copies of 'Lovey' to 30,000 of 'Lick' – saw them perilously close to a less than voluntary return to the indie sector.

Dando put it down to musical schizophrenia that meant they were difficult to market. "We don't really have a specific genre," he insisted. "The biggest non-compliment I can think of when I see other bands is that they've turned into late-period Ramones – all their songs are at the same speed and at the same pitch." That patently wasn't The Lemonheads. In addition, there may well have been shades of the backlash that faces every indie band when they get too big for their label – some believe you can substitute 'boots' for label. But there were other factors at work too, notably Jesse's departure which hadn't helped the band promote it.

looked as if 'It's A Shame About Ray' might sink in similar fashion... until a second lucky cover version fired the starting gun and propelled The Lemonheads into long-awaited orbit.

Originally released in 1968, the catchy 'Mrs Robinson' had gone Top 5 for Simon and Garfunkel back in the days when both had hair. It was the theme tune for The Graduate, the film that thrust Dustin Hoffman into the limelight – and with almost uncanny timing, The Lemonheads' version heralded the film's debut on home video.

"It's just a weird little vehicle to reach some more people," Evan explained. "People know that I write OK songs, so y'know... I like to sing, y'know? I love writing songs but it's with it for me to just get up and sing any old song." As for the supposed coincidence, "We recorded it because these people bought the rights to The Graduate and wanted to get the movie to some flannel-ripped-jeans-wearing people." (In fact, it was one of Evando's favourite films.) And as for the chances of 'Mrs Robinson' becoming a Lemonheads' stage staple, these were slim indeed. "I'm never gonna play it again in a couple of months: it was just a fluke... it's gonna be over."

If he wasn't openly proud of their rendition, perhaps that was because the song was actually recorded in just a couple of takes after a festival appearance in Germany when the band was hardly at its freshest. It was also the first Lemonheads release to feature bassist Nic Dalton, who'd been flown in from Oz to take over the bass after the

second-time-round departure of Jesse Peretz.

Now, contrary to what Neighbours and Home And Away fans might think, there's plenty going on in the land Down Under – and most of it seemed to revolve around Dalton. He ran the label, Half A Cow, for which Tom Morgan's current band Smudge, releases records; less than coincidentally, he managed a bookshop called Half A Cow in Sydney and more recently ran the branch in Canberra.

And that wasn't all. He had his own band, Godstar (with Evan occasionally on drums), found time to play with other Aussie bands like Sneeze, Sidewinder and Hippy Drivel and ran a music publishing company.

But the spotlight was still firmly

aimed elsewhere. The thousands for whom 'Mrs Robinson' was their first introduction to The Lemonheads bought the sound, the attitude – and, it has to be said, the good looks – of Evan Dando.

They bought into a success story that clearly had a long way to run. But the next chapter would be nearly a year in coming. The 'sleeper' effect of the album, to which 'Mrs Robinson' would be added in later pressings, meant that just when they should have been taking a break to write their next long-player The Lemonheads would be busily promoting the last one. That Guns N'Roses had endured a similar problem with their 'Appetite For Destruction' was little consolation for the man whose mastery of the 'Sweet Child O'Mine' riff was rivalled only by Slash...

Atlantic were doing their best, as vice-president Danny Goldberg explained. "I had to find him new management... until then, Evan had dealt with the business side of the band. He was well liked, but wasn't very good at the mechanics of the industry." As for the singer himself, he confessed, "Sometimes I just can't put two and two together," recalling how he'd found himself stranded at London's Heathrow Airport when he fell asleep waiting for an outbound flight. Having waited so long for success, he couldn't afford to miss the boat now...

The pressures of the past months had clearly got to the man who now, single-handedly, steered The Lemonheads' fortunes. By the beginning of 1993, they'd clocked up seven tours of Europe, four tours of the States and three tours of Australia, all in just three years. And all the signs were that Dando was buckling under the strain.

Atlantic expected an album for the Christmas market, but Evan was patently going to find it difficult to deliver. "I partied too much for too long here in LA," he told New Musical Express, "and it fucked up my voice." He confessed to 'dabbling' in hard drugs, claiming "the pressure probably led me into the drug problems in the first place."

The whole sorry story, he claimed, started when he played at the opening of actor and friend Johnny Depp's club. "We partied a bit, and that was the beginning of (a) really bad weekend. Then I started partying too much. I was hanging out with a lot of people and they were doing a lot of drugs... a lot of people have the feeling about drugs that they

National Theatre in London's Kilburn. Kicking off with a tried and tested trio from 'Ray' – 'Confetti', 'Rudderless' and 'Alison's Starting To Happen' – that brought the capacity crowd to life, the trio of Dando, Dalton and Ryan laid down a powerful yet pleasing pop sound it would have taken half a dozen lesser musicians to conjure up.

make life better and, sure, you feel good for a little while, but really drugs make life worse in the end. You don't have your normal glee left at all, you just have that very reliable, unnatural high."

Yet for an hour or so in the spotlight, away from all possible temptation, Dando and his cohorts could still cut it, as they showed in their early 1993 show at the

A deft change of pace incorporated 'It's A Shame About Ray', 'My Drug Buddy' and 'Ride With Me' before 'Kitchen' kicked in, its heavier sound marking the start of a gallop towards the set's climax as a new song, 'Style', offered a perplexing dilemma in its chorus: 'I don't wanna get stoned, but I don't wanna not get stoned.'

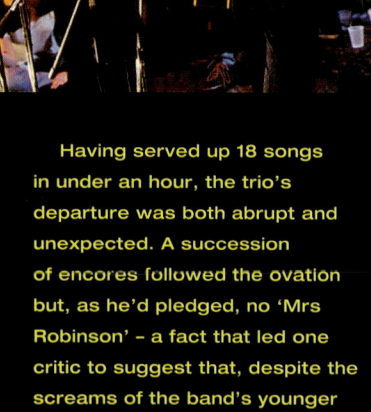

Having served up 18 songs in under an hour, the trio's departure was both abrupt and unexpected. A succession of encores followed the ovation but, as he'd pledged, no 'Mrs Robinson' – a fact that led one critic to suggest that, despite the screams of the band's younger fans, Evan Dando "is still nobody's cuddly toy".

A new album just couldn't wait indefinitely, and the trio headed back to the studios to face the music. But British festival slots had already been slated for Glastonbury (where their performance of 'Hannah And Gabi' made it onto a compilation CD, 'In A Field Of Their Own') and August at Reading: the latter, in particular, provided a welcome break from their endeavours. Amidst all the rumours, the band's appearance was eagerly awaited... and Dando didn't let fans or critics down, making his entrance in a flower-print cotton dress, hair in two bunches and suspenders drawn on with felt-tip pen.

He flew back from Reading in supersonic style on Concorde ("I can't wait... I'm so excited") to finish the album. It's understood he behaved rather better than on the plane over to Glastonbury, when a stewardess had apparently attempted to have him removed from the flight. "I dropped a Mandrax ten minutes before I got on the plane so I was feeling a bit silly," he explained backstage.

"I started asking her about her mother's Christian name and she had me ejected. I wasn't violent or threatening... she didn't have a sense of humour."

But come October, critics and fans alike were smiling. Against all odds, 'Come On Feel The Lemonheads' was adjudged by all to be worth the wait – but it was a singular album indeed. All the studio chat, unexpected silences and the like remained unedited,

adding to the idiosyncratic, intimate air. But it was an album that had been produced under pressure, and with recording stretching through August and a release date of October 11 approaching at the speed of a runaway train, it had been touch and go.

Yet all was not lost, as co-producer Joe Robb explained. "Evan's a non-linear guy. There might be nothing going on one day, or two days. Then he'll come in and in two hours he'll do so much, he comes in with these flashes of genius. It's really neat." Something else that probably didn't help was the planeloads of journalists flown in to interview Evan as the sessions reached their height. His voice was so ravaged by the effects of his excessive lifestyle that he had to answer their questions via a pen and paper, saving his best efforts for recording tape.

Strangely for someone who's chopped and changed his musicians almost at will, Evan's approach to the studio never varied. He enters it almost unprepared, armed only with his trusty Gibson SG electric and Martin acoustic guitars. ("We once tried to get him to play another guitar apart from the SG," said his former producer, "and he refused.")

Gram Parsons, the lead singer of country-rock pioneers the Flying Burrito Brothers and one of rock's most tragic losses, had long been quoted by Dando as a (somewhat dangerous) role model. Joe Robb believes that "Evan recognised the similarities without ever knowing the guy. Although Gram was in the middle of the music business round here,

he was completely isolated from it." That certainly fitted a man who owned neither a car nor a fixed abode...

Another former Burrito, 'Sneeky' Pete Kleinow, clearly believed Evan's sincerity, adding his sneeky steel guitar to 'Big Gay Heart'. It's doubtful, though, if he heard the lyrics to the final version, which caused a furore – and more – when Radio 1 played the track in 1994. "It's anti gay bashing," explained the author. "A non-violence song. The title came from Johnny Depp, who described his place as a big gay house. It has that happy meaning, too." He eventually re-recorded the track for airplay purposes, changing "suck my dick" to the "duck my sick", but by then the damage had been done.

Interestingly, another dissenting voice closer to home was Nic Dalton who like David Ryan only heard the completed album on release. He believed the pedal steel guitar ruined the song, something that shook Dando when he first heard it. Whether this meant future Lemonheads efforts will be more democratic affairs remains to be seen...

Three of the songs had already turned up in acoustic demo versions on single B-sides, which according to taste added to their familiar appeal or suggested limits to the repertoire, while 'Being Around' had featured in the live set for some while now. Elsewhere among the 15 tracks, the music ran the gamut of musical reference points in typically bewildering Dando style.

He'd written 'I'll Do It Anyway' with Belinda Carlisle in mind, so it had seemed logical to get the blonde Californian former Go Go to sing backing vocals. Ditto Motown funk legend Rick James for 'Rick James Style', which retained all the power of the stage original that had hypnotised his London audience earlier in the year.

As ever, there was many a story behind the songs. 'Favourite T' was about his ex-girlfriend Hannah – her again! – who went off with an Austrian boy (translated to Danish in the lyric to summon up the right image) and took many of Evan's most treasured clothes with her. "Don't you think that's a thing a lot of people have been through?" he asked one interviewer plaintively. "At first it doesn't matter, then it starts eating away at something..."

As 'Come On Feel The Lemonheads' (its title borrowed from a Seventies Slade stomper) faded away into the distance with an impassioned rendition of Cole Porter's 'Miss Otis Regrets', Evan Dando summed up his feelings about the whole experience.

"I felt so much pressure about the record. It was like, oh wow, I've got to do a record that everyone's going to really love. When I quit the drugs, I realised that all I had to do was make a record that I really, like, loved, and that's it's own reward... any monetary gain from the record is incidental. For me," he concluded, "it's about making music that makes me happy and other people happy."

And something that would make his drummer happy would be less talk about drugs! Though he played in a local Boston band,

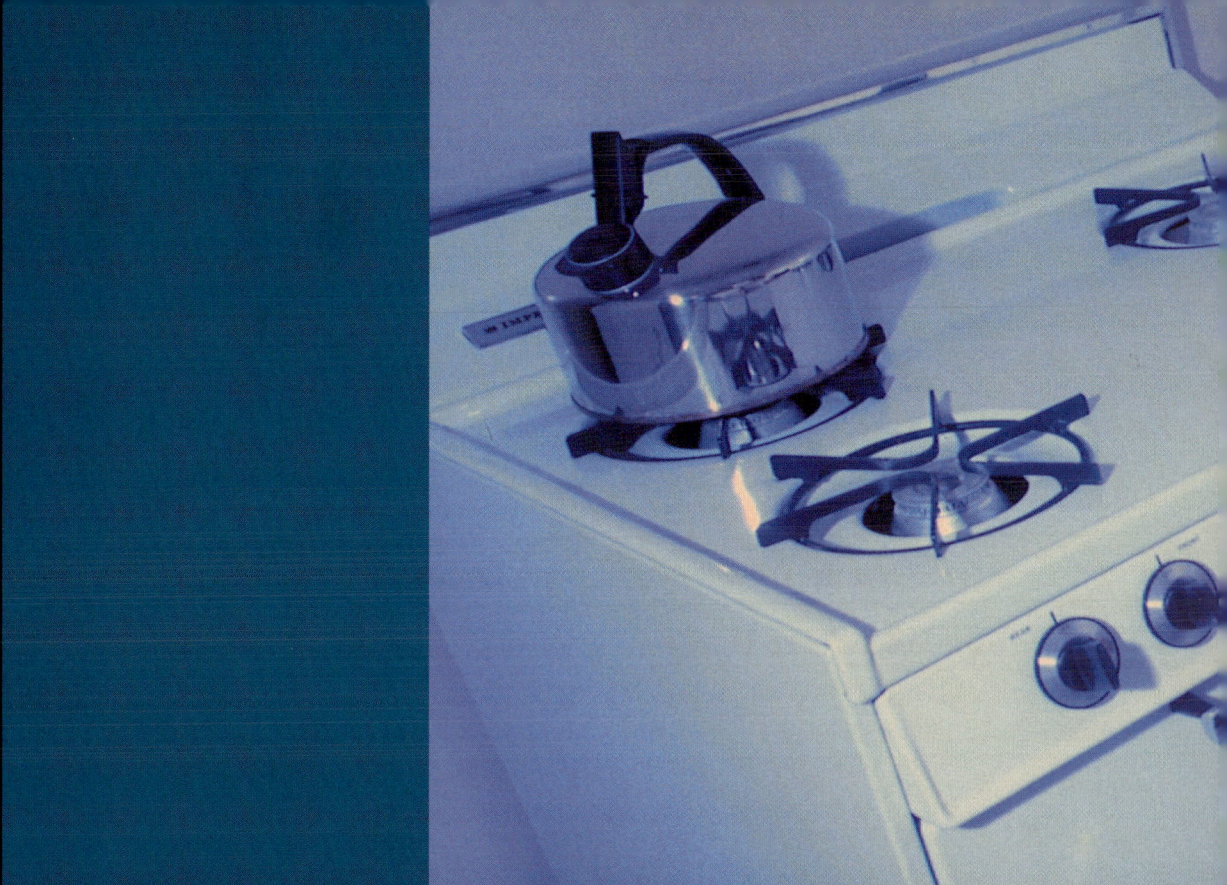

Fuzzy, during his time off, The Lemonheads were clearly his meal ticket. "I need a job," he told a British magazine interviewer. "And I don't want to see Evan hurt himself." As for his partner in rhythm Nic Dalton, the new album was nothing new: "much like the stuff I've been playing since 1984 in the Half A Cow scene, that's what gave him the new direction."

Reviewers were less grudging in their praise for 'Come On Feel The Lemonheads'. "A Greatest Hits set from the first chord," enthused Vox magazine's reviewer who, in his enthusiasm, likened Dando to both Lennon and McCartney. Q reckoned the album was "as lovable as it was listenable: The Lemonheads have come into bloom like a daisy pushing through the surface in the post-grunge wasteland."

▼ JULIANA HATFIELD

So far, so good with the album. On the singles front, 'Into Your Arms' (written by Oz-rock bassist Robyn St Claire) and the poppy 'It's About Time' turned out to be rather safer bets than 'Big Gay Heart' when it came to airplay – though it's certain that no DJ who wants to keep his job will ever again spin a Lemonheads record unheard. But it's just as sure there'll be plenty more sounds to savour as long as Evan keeps his self-destructive urges in check. "Don't do drugs, kids, drink tea instead," he insisted on stage in late 1993. "It soothes your voice and keeps you high."

Did he worry, though, that the inspiration might dry up with the drugs supply? Not at all, he claimed, though he admitted, "The track record of people who straighten up and continue to sing their hearts out is not a good one... but we'll see. Going out and playing, performing, is better straight... Listen kids, you can get the same effect from doing a painting with a strobe light on and playing the guitar at the same time." And sucking a Lemonhead sweet? Coincidentally and perhaps ironically, the confectionery's side flap now instructed purchasers to "say no to drugs".

If the recording sessions had been widely publicised, The Lemonheads' British tour which kicked off at Cambridge on October 7 was the highest-profile affair they'd yet enjoyed. Or should that be endured? Fresh from Dando's Stateside revelations, scribes were as alert backstage for the presence of artificial stimulants as for musical edification.

Thankfully for Evan, Juliana was around to lend moral as well as musical support, opening

the shows with the Juliana Hatfield Three. Prospects of a conventional romance, though, remained limited. "She wouldn't want to be in a monogamous relationship with me, she's very independent. But she doesn't like the way my flirting behaviour looks... sometimes I think it's pretty gross too! I just like girls and I want love badly..."

Strangely, one of the most publicised gigs was not a public one at all. When the kids of a comprehensive school in Pontefract, West Yorkshire, asked The Lemonheads to come and play in the assembly hall, the media came too, with children's TV host Andi Peters and a camera crew recording proceedings. And although young kids were seen swaying sweetly with oversize 'My Drug Buddy' T-shirts, the only Coke to be consumed was the black, fizzy variety. "So he's been talking about crack in the NME, shock, horror," opined one teacher. "A lot of the kids at this school have come across worse than that before."

They'd also come across bands before, Kingmaker, The Wonder Stuff and The Levellers among those who'd crossed the academic portals, but all teachers agreed that The Lemonheads beat the competition hands down. Maybe a song like 'Stove' could be considered a home economics anthem... though the massed community singing when Evan's voice started to show the strain later in the set seemed to suggest The Lemonheads' 11-plus fan following was already alive and well.

The release of 'Into Your Arms' (backed up with acoustic tracks 'Little Black Egg' and 'Learning The Game' unavailable elsewhere) to coincide with the tour was heralded by full-page music-press ads featuring pictures of Evan on a plane, airline food and a window seat. It had been a jet-set life, all right, and the pace didn't look to be letting up just yet... even if he wasn't falling asleep at airports these days!

Ben Deily, meanwhile, had released his first single with The Pods on the tiny Stone Records label. Entitled 'It's A Bummer About Bourbie' (Dando's youthful nickname), it betrayed a certain and entirely forgivable irritation that the group he'd co-founded had taken off without him. But even The Lemonheads' own version of Pete Best had the grace to admit that "If there was any justice, Evan should be the one to make it, because he wanted it more than anyone else. It was very important to him, and he just plugged away at it."

Though there's no doubting who now called the shots, the ext‍ Lemonheads family still included Jesse Peretz, who now fulfilled his muse by shooting their videos and taking their publicity photos. It may yet encompass another musician, for concert purposes at least. "Sometimes I think we might have to get another guitar player, because our shows are getting kind of big. I think I'm gonna need another player so I can relax a little more." A keyboardist, perhaps? "I don't think we'll be ge‍ one of those."

It seemed likely, however, that The Lemonheads would remain Evan and supporting cast, especially when Nic expressed an

understandable desire to get back to doing his own thing in Australia. "We like the fact that we've helped Evan become a big pop star," he commented on behalf of his countrymen, "because he's also helped get our music get known around the world. But the bigger The Lemonheads get the more I want to get away from them. It's just not my scene."

No matter who might be involved, the future for The Lemonheads seemed as infinite as Dando's own possibilities. "I don't believe this bullshit that every song has been written," he said – and as long as his personal life feeds his muse you can believe it. But there's a new ambition behind the easy-going façade.

"I really wanna get my music heard," he insisted. "For the first time, I feel a bit ambitious... only for a couple of years, mind you. I'm planning on getting real lazy in the not too distant future. But I'm not that good at sitting around. I get kinda crazy and depressed when I don't work. I'm of the opinion that human beings are meant to be doing something." Part Julian Cope, part Morrissey but one hundred per cent himself, Evan Dando will continue to lead with his chin, serving up 'good copy' to the rock press and even better sounds to his passionate public. Having drawn back from the edge, it seemed unlikely he'll ever record an album in as drawn-out and convoluted a way as 'Ray' came together: "Next time I make a record," he insisted, "I'm gonna make it in about a month."

Beyond that, who knows?

"I think I'll be ready in a year or two to meet a really nice girl and get married or something, and have kids." Go ahead, Evan...the world wants your babies!

Discography

Singles

Luka / Strange / Mad
Taang! 31 (7") April 1989 (US-only release)

Different Drum / Paint
Roughneck HYPE 3 (7") June 1990

Different Drum / Paint / Ride With Me
Roughneck 12 HYPE 3 (12") June 1990

Different Drum / Paint / Ride With Me
Roughneck HYPE 3 CD (CD) June 1990

**Gonna Get Along Without Ya Now /
Half The Time**
Atlantic A 7709 (7") September 1991

**Patience And Prudence: Gonna Get
Along Without Ya Now / Stove(Remix) /
Half The Time / Step By Step**
Atlantic TA 7709 (12") September 1991

It's A Shame About Ray / Shakey Ground
Atlantic A 7423 (7") October 1992

It's A Shame About Ray / Shakey Ground
Atlantic A 7423C (Cassette) October 1992

**It's A Shame About Ray / Shakey Ground /
Dawn Can't Decide / The Turnpike Down**
Atlantic A 7423TE (10") October 1992

**It's A Shame About Ray / Shakey Ground /
Dawn Can't Decide / The Turnpike Down**
Atlantic A 7423CD (CD) October 1992

Mrs Robinson / Being Around
Atlantic A 7401 (7") November 1992

Mrs Robinson / Being Around
Atlantic A 7401C (Cassette) November 1992

**Mrs Robinson / Being Around / Divan /
Into Your Arms**
Atlantic A 7401TE (10") November 1992

**Mrs Robinson / Being Around / Divan /
Into Your Arms**
Atlantic A 7401CD (CD) November 1992

Confetti (Remix) / My Drug Buddy
Atlantic A 7430 (7") January 1993

Confetti (Remix) / My Drug Buddy
Atlantic A 7430C (Cassette) January 1993

**Confetti (Remix) / My Drug Buddy /
Ride With Me (Live In Boston) /
Confetti (Acoustic)**
Atlantic A 7430TE (10") January 1993

**Confetti (Remix) / My Drug Buddy /
Ride With Me (Live In Boston) /
Confetti (Acoustic)**
Atlantic A 7430CD (CD) January 1993

Different Drum / Paint / Ride With Me
Roughneck HYPE 3T (12" reissue) February 1993

Different Drum / Paint / Ride With Me
Roughneck HYPE 3CD (CD reissue) February 1993

**It's A Shame About Ray / Different Drum
(Acoustic) / Alison's Starting To Happen
(Live) / Rockin' Stroll (Live)**
Atlantic A 5764TE (10") March 1993

**It's A Shame About Ray / Alison's
Starting To Happen**
Atlantic A 5764C (Cassette) March 1993

**It's A Shame About Ray (Live) /
Confetti (Live) / Mallo Cup (Live) /
Rudderless (Live)**
Atlantic 5764CDX (CD) March 1993

**It's A Shame About Ray (Album
Version) / Alison's Starting To Happen
(Evan Acoustic) / Stove (Evan Acoustic) /
Different Drum (Evan Acoustic)**
Atlantic A 5764CD (CD) April 1993

Into Your Arms / Miss Otis Regrets
Atlantic A 7302 (7") October 1993

Into Your Arms / Miss Otis Regrets
Atlantic A 7302C (Cassette) October 1993

**Into Your Arms / Miss Otis Regrets /
Little Black Egg / Learning The Game**
Atlantic A 7302TE (10") October 1993

**Into Your Arms / Miss Otis Regrets /
Little Black Egg / Learning The Game**
Atlantic A 7302CD (CD) October 1993

**It's About Time / Rick James
Acoustic Style**
Atlantic A 7296 (7") November 1993

**It's About Time / Rick James
Acoustic Style**
Atlantic A 7296C (Cassette) November 1993

**It's About Time / Rick James Acoustic
Style / Down About It (Acoustic) /
Big Gay Heart (Demo)**
Atlantic A 7296TE (10") November 1993

**It's About Time / Rick James Acoustic
Style / Down About It (Acoustic) /
Big Gay Heart (Demo)**
Atlantic A 7296CD (CD) November 1993

Albums

Hate Your Friends
I Don't Wanna / 3 94 / Nothing True /
Second Chance / Sneakyville /
Amazing Grace / Belt / Hate Your
Friends / Don't Tell Yourself It's OK /
Uhhh / Fed Up / Rat Velvet / F*cked Up
World Service SERVM 004 May 1988

Creator
Burying Ground / Sunday / Clang Bang
Clang / Out / Your Home Is Where
You're Happy / Falling / Die Right Now /
Two Weeks In Another Town / Plaster
Caster / Come To The Window / Take
Her Down / Postcard / Live Without
World Service SERV 001 September 1988

Lick
Mallo Cup / Glad I Don't Know /
7 Powers / A Circle Of One / Cazzo Di
Ferro / Anyway / Luka / Come Back D.A. /
I Am A Rabbit / Sad Girl / Ever
World Service SERV / SERV CD 007 May 1989

Create Your Friends
I Don't Wanna / 3 94 / Nothing True /
Second Chance / Sneakyville / Amazing
Grace / Belt / Hate Your Friends / Don't
Tell Yourself It's OK / Uhhh / Fed Up /
Rat Velvet / F*cked Up / Burying
Ground / Sunday / Clang Bang Clang /
Out / Your Home Is Where You're
Happy / Falling / Die Right Now / Two
Weeks In Another Town / Plaster
Caster / Come To The Window /
Take Her Down / Postcard / Live
Without / Glad I Don't Know / I Like
To / I Am A Rabbit / So I F*cked Up
Taang! T15 / T23 1990 (US-only release)

Lovey
Ballarat / Half The Time / Year Of
The Cat / Ride With Me / Li'l Seed /
Stove / Come Downstairs / Left For
Dead / Brass Buttons / (The) Door
Atlantic 7567821371/2 October 1990

It's A Shame About Ray
Rockin' Stroll / Confetti / It's A Shame
About Ray / Rudderless / Buddy /
The Turnpike Down / Bit Part / Alison's
Starting To Happen / Hannah &
Gabi / Kitchen / Ceiling Fan In My
Spoon / Frank Mills / Mrs Robinson
(CD only)
Atlantic 7567823971/2 July 1992

Come On Feel The Lemonheads
Great Big No / Into Your Arms / It's
About Time / Down About It / Paid To
Smile / Big Gay Heart / Style / Rest
Assured / Dawn Can't Decide / I'll Do
It Anyway / Rick James Style / Being
Around / Favourite T / You Can Take
It Away With You / Jello Fund
Atlantic 7567825371/2 October 1993

EPs

**Laughing All The Way To The
Cleaners:**
Glad I Don't Know / I Like To / I Am
A Rabbit / So I F*cked Up
Amory Arms 1/2 / Huh-Bag 1 (7") 1986
(US-only release)

Favourite Spanish Dishes:
Different Drum / Paint / Ride With Me /
Skulls / Step By Step
Atlantic 786088-2 (CD) 1990 (US-only release)

DISCOGRAPHICAL NOTE
Outside the UK, individual Lemonheads /
Evan Dando tracks have also appeared
on everything from various artist
samplers to magazine-mounted
Flexidiscs and fan club EPs. Dando
himself has guested with groups as
diverse as Blake Babies, Speed Nigs,
Smudge and Godstar, though not
always as a vocalist.

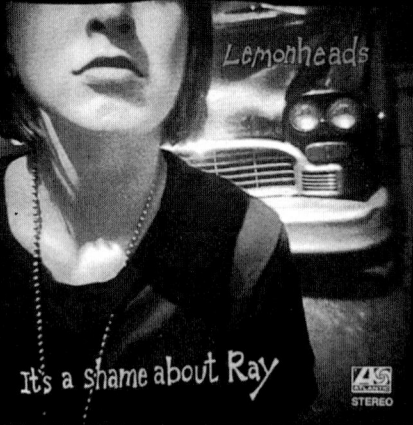